Pippa Passes by Robert Browning

A DRAMA

From Bells and Pomegranates Number I

Robert Browning is one of the most significant Victorian Poets and, of course, English Poetry.

Much of his reputation is based upon his mastery of the dramatic monologue although his talents encompassed verse plays and even a well-regarded essay on Shelley during a long and prolific career.

He was born on May 7th, 1812 in Walmouth, London. Much of his education was home based and Browning was an eclectic and studious student, learning several languages and much else across a myriad of subjects, interests and passions.

Browning's early career began promisingly. The fragment from his intended long poem Pauline brought him to the attention of Dante Gabriel Rossetti, and was followed by Paracelsus, which was praised by both William Wordsworth and Charles Dickens. In 1840 the difficult Sordello, which was seen as willfully obscure, brought his career almost to a standstill.

Despite these artistic and professional difficulties his personal life was about to become immensely fulfilling. He began a relationship with, and then married, the older and better known Elizabeth Barrett. This new foundation served to energise his writings, his life and his career.

During their time in Italy they both wrote much of their best work. With her untimely death in 1861 he returned to London and thereafter began several further major projects.

The collection Dramatis Personae (1864) and the book-length epic poem The Ring and the Book (1868-69) were published and well received; his reputation as a venerated English poet now assured.

Robert Browning died in Venice on December 12th, 1889.

Index of Contents

PREFACE

Sordello did not prove commercially successful, and Browning was reluctant to go on publishing his poetry at his father's expense. "One day," Mr. Gosse says, "as the poet was discussing the matter with Mr. Edward Moxon, the publisher, the latter remarked that at that time he was bringing out some editions of the old Elizabethan dramatists in a comparatively cheap form, and that if Mr. Browning would consent to print his poems as pamphlets, using this cheap type, the expense would be very inconsiderable." Browning accepted the suggestion at once and began the issue of a cheap series of pamphlets, each sixteen octavo pages in double column, printed on poor paper and sold first for a sixpence each, the price afterward being raised to a shilling and then to half a crown. The series consisted of eight numbers under the general fanciful title Bells and Pomegranates. Apparently the passage in Exodus xxviii. 33, "And beneath upon the hem of it [the priest's robe] thou shalt make pomegranates of blue, and of purple, and of scarlet, round about the hem thereof; and bells of gold between them round about," suggested the title, but as all sorts of speculations sprang up about its significance, Browning appended the following note to the eighth and final number of the series:—

"Here ends my first series of Bells and Pomegranates, and I take the opportunity of explaining, in reply to inquiries, that I only meant by that title to indicate an endeavor towards something like an alteration, or mixture, of music with discoursing, sound with sense, poetry with thought; which looks too ambitious, thus expressed, so the symbol was preferred. It is little to the purpose, that such is actually one of the most familiar of the many Rabbinical (and Patristic) acceptations of the phrase; because I confess that, letting authority alone, I suppose the bare words, in such juxtaposition, would sufficiently convey the desired meaning. 'Faith and good works' is another fancy, for instance, and perhaps no easier to arrive at; yet Giotto placed a pomegranate fruit in the hand of Dante, and Raffaello crowned his Theology (in the Camera della Segnatura) with blossoms of the same; as if the Bellari and Vasari would be sure to come after, and explain that it was merely 'simbolo delle buone opere—il qual Pomogranato fu però usato nelle veste del Pontefice appresso gli Ebrei.'

"R. B."

The first number of Bells and Pomegranates contained Pippa Passes. It was published in 1841 and was introduced by the following dedicatory preface:—

ADVERTISEMENT

Two or three years ago I wrote a Play, about which the chief matter I much care to recollect at present is, that a Pitfull of good-natured people applauded it: ever since, I have been desirous of doing something in the same way that should better reward their attention. What follows, I mean for the first of a series of Dramatical Pieces, to come out at intervals; and I amuse myself by fancying that the cheap mode in which they appear, will for once help me to a sort of Pit-audience again. Of course such a work must go on no longer than it is liked; and to provide against a too certain and but too possible contingency, let me hasten to say now—what, if I were sure of success, I would try to say circumstantially enough at the close—that I dedicate my best intentions most admiringly to the Author of Ion—most affectionately to Sergeant Talfourd.

ROBERT BROWNING.

The phrases in the closing sentence were afterward used by Browning as a dedication when he discarded the advertisement in the collective editions of his poems.

PIPPA PASSES

PERSONS
PIPPA
OTTIMA
SEBALD
Foreign Students
GOTTLIEB
SCHRAMM
JULES
PHENE
Austrian Police
BLUPHOCKS
LUIGI and his mother
Poor Girls
MONSIGNOR and his attendants

INTRODUCTION

NEW YEAR'S DAY AT ASOLO IN THE TREVISAN

A large mean airy chamber. A girl, **PIPPA**, from the silk-mills, springing out of bed.

DAY!
Faster and more fast,
O'er night's brim, day boils at last:
Boils, pure gold, o'er the cloud-cup's brim
Where spurting and suppressed it lay,
For not a froth-flake touched the rim
Of yonder gap in the solid gray
Of the eastern cloud, an hour away;
But forth one wavelet, then another, curled,
Till the whole sunrise, not to be suppressed,
Rose, reddened, and its seething breast
Flickered in bounds, grew gold, then overflowed the world.

Oh Day, if I squander a wavelet of thee,
A mite of my twelve-hours' treasure,
The least of thy gazes or glances,
(Be they grants thou art bound to or gifts above measure)
One of thy choices or one of thy chances,
(Be they tasks God imposed thee or freaks at thy pleasure)
—My Day, if I squander such labor or leisure,
Then shame fall on Asolo, mischief on me!

Thy long blue solemn hours serenely flowing,
Whence earth, we feel, gets steady help and good—
Thy fitful sunshine-minutes, coming, going,
As if earth turned from work in gamesome mood—
All shall be mine! But thou must treat me not
As prosperous ones are treated, those who live
At hand here, and enjoy the higher lot,
In readiness to take what thou wilt give,
And free to let alone what thou refusest;
For, Day, my holiday, if thou ill-usest
Me, who am only Pippa,—old-year's sorrow,
Cast off last night, will come again to-morrow:
Whereas, if thou prove gentle, I shall borrow
Sufficient strength of thee for new-year's sorrow.
All other men and women that this earth
Belongs to, who all days alike possess,
Make general plenty cure particular dearth,
Get more joy one way, if another, less:
Thou art my single day, God lends to leaven
What were all earth else, with a feel of heaven,—
Sole light that helps me through the year, thy sun's!
Try now! Take Asolo's Four Happiest Ones—
And let thy morning rain on that superb
Great haughty Ottima; can rain disturb
Her Sebald's homage? All the while thy rain
Beats fiercest on her shrub-house window-pane
He will but press the closer, breathe more warm
Against her cheek; how should she mind the storm?
And, morning past, if mid-day shed a gloom
O'er Jules and Phene,—what care bride and groom
Save for their dear selves? 'T is their marriage-day;
And while they leave church and go home their way,
Hand clasping hand, within each breast would be
Sunbeams and pleasant weather spite of thee.
Then, for another trial, obscure thy eve
With mist,—will Luigi and his mother grieve—
The lady and her child, unmatched, forsooth,
She in her age, as Luigi in his youth,
For true content? The cheerful town, warm, close
And safe, the sooner that thou art morose,
Receives them. And yet once again, outbreak
In storm at night on Monsignor, they make
Such stir about,—whom they expect from Rome
To visit Asolo, his brothers' home,
And say here masses proper to release
A soul from pain,—what storm dares hurt his peace?
Calm would he pray, with his own thoughts to ward
Thy thunder off, nor want the angels' guard.
But Pippa—just one such mischance would spoil
Her day that lightens the next twelvemonth's toil
At wearisome silk-winding, coil on coil!

And here I let time slip for naught!
Aha, you foolhardy sunbeam, caught
With a single splash from my ewer!
You that would mock the best pursuer,
Was my basin over-deep?
One splash of water ruins you asleep,
And up, up, fleet your brilliant bits
Wheeling and counterwheeling,
Reeling, broken beyond healing:
Now grow together on the ceiling!
That will task your wits.
Whoever it was quenched fire first, hoped to see
Morsel after morsel flee
As merrily, as giddily ...
Meantime, what lights my sunbeam on,
Where settles by degrees the radiant cripple?
Oh, is it surely blown, my martagon?
New-blown and ruddy as St. Agnes' nipple,
Plump as the flesh-bunch on some Turk bird's poll!
Be sure if corals, branching 'neath the ripple
Of ocean, bud there,—fairies watch unroll
Such turban-flowers; I say, such lamps disperse
Thick red flame through that dusk green universe!
I am queen of thee, floweret!
And each fleshy blossom
Preserve I not—(safer
Than leaves that embower it,
Or shells that embosom)
—From weevil and chafer?
Laugh through my pane then; solicit the bee;
Gibe him, be sure; and, in midst of thy glee,
Love thy queen, worship me!

—Worship whom else? For am I not, this day,
Whate'er I please? What shall I please to-day?
My morn, noon, eve and night—how spend my day?
To-morrow I must be Pippa who winds silk,
The whole year round, to earn just bread and milk:
But, this one day, I have leave to go,
And play out my fancy's fullest games;
I may fancy all day—and it shall be so—
That I taste of the pleasures, am called by the names
Of the Happiest Four in our Asolo!

See! Up the hillside yonder, through the morning,
Some one shall love me, as the world calls love:
I am no less than Ottima, take warning!
The gardens, and the great stone house above,
And other house for shrubs, all glass in front,
Are mine; where Sebald steals, as he is wont,
To court me, while old Luca yet reposes:

And therefore, till the shrub-house door un-closes,
I ... what now?—give abundant cause for prate
About me—Ottima, I mean—of late,
Too bold, too confident she'll still face down
The spitefullest of talkers in our town.
How we talk in the little town below!
But love, love, love—there's better love, I know!
This foolish love was only day's first offer;
I choose my next love to defy the scoffer:
For do not our Bride and Bridegroom sally
Out of Possagno church at noon?
Their house looks over Orcana valley:
Why should not I be the bride as soon
As Ottima? For I saw, beside,
Arrive last night that little bride—
Saw, if you call it seeing her, one flash
Of the pale snow-pure cheek and black bright tresses,
Blacker than all except the black eyelash;
I wonder she contrives those lids no dresses!
—So strict was she, the veil
Should cover close her pale
Pure cheeks—a bride to look at and scarce touch,
Scarce touch, remember, Jules! For are not such
Used to be tended, flower-like, every feature,
As if one's breath would fray the lily of a creature?
A soft and easy life these ladies lead:
Whiteness in us were wonderful indeed.
Oh, save that brow its virgin dimness,
Keep that foot its lady primness,
Let those ankles never swerve
From their exquisite reserve,
Yet have to trip along the streets like me,
All but naked to the knee!
How will she ever grant her Jules a bliss
So startling as her real first infant kiss?
Oh, no—not envy, this!

—Not envy, sure!—for if you gave me
Leave to take or to refuse,
In earnest, do you think I 'd choose
That sort of new love to enslave me?
Mine should have lapped me round from the beginning;
As little fear of losing it as winning:
Lovers grow cold, men learn to hate their wives,
And only parents' love can last our lives.
At eve the Son and Mother, gentle pair,
Commune inside our turret: what prevents
My being Luigi? While that mossy lair
Of lizards through the winter-time is stirred
With each to each imparting sweet intents
For this new-year, as brooding bird to bird—

(For I observe of late, the evening walk
Of Luigi and his mother, always ends
Inside our ruined turret, where they talk,
Calmer than lovers, yet more kind than friends)
—Let me be cared about, kept out of harm,
And schemed for, safe in love as with a charm;
Let me be Luigi! If I only knew
What was my mother's face—my father, too!
Nay, if you come to that, best love of all
Is God's; then why not have God's love befall
Myself as, in the palace by the Dome,
Monsignor?—who to-night will bless the home
Of his dead brother; and God bless in turn
That heart which beats, those eyes which mildly burn
With love for all men! I, to-night at least,
Would be that holy and beloved priest.

Now wait!—even I already seem to share
In God's love: what does New-year's hymn declare?
What other meaning do these verses bear?

All service ranks the same with God:
If now, as formerly he trod
Paradise, his presence fills
Our earth, each only as God wills
Can work—God's puppets, best and worst,
Are we; there is no last nor first.

Say not "a small event!" Why "small"?
Costs it more pain that this, ye call
A "great event," should come to pass,
Than that? Untwine me from the mass
Of deeds which make up life, one deed
Power shall fall short in or exceed!

And more of it, and more of it!—oh yes—
I will pass each, and see their happiness,
And envy none—being just as great, no doubt,
Useful to men, and dear to God, as they!
A pretty thing to care about
So mightily, this single holiday!
But let the sun shine! Wherefore repine?
—With thee to lead me, O Day of mine,
Down the grass path gray with dew,
Under the pine-wood, blind with boughs,
Where the swallow never flew
Nor yet cicala dared carouse—
No, dared carouse!

[She enters the street.

Up the Hillside, inside the Shrub-house. Luca's Wife **OTTIMA**, and her Paramour, the German **SEBALD**.

SEBALD [sings]
Let the watching lids wink!
Day's ablaze with eyes, think!
Deep into the night, drink!

OTTIMA
Night? Such may be your Rhine-land nights, perhaps;
But this blood-red beam through the shutter's chink
—We call such light, the morning: let us see!
Mind how you grope your way, though! How these tall
Naked geraniums straggle! Push the lattice
Behind that frame!—Nay, do I bid you?—Sebald,
It shakes the dust down on me! Why, of course
The slide-bolt catches. Well, are you content,
Or must I find you something else to spoil?
Kiss and be friends, my Sebald! Is 't full morning?
Oh, don't speak then!

SEBALD
Ay, thus it used to be!
Ever your house was, I remember, shut
Till mid-day; I observed that, as I strolled
On mornings through the vale here; country girls
Were noisy, washing garments in the brook,
Hinds drove the slow white oxen up the hills:
But no, your house was mute, would ope no eye!
And wisely: you were plotting one thing there,
Nature, another outside. I looked up—
Rough white wood shutters, rusty iron bars,
Silent as death, blind in a flood of light.
Oh, I remember!—and the peasants laughed
And said, "The old man sleeps with the young wife."
This house was his, this chair, this window—his.

OTTIMA
Ah, the clear morning! I can see Saint Mark's;
That black streak is the belfry. Stop: Vicenza
Should lie ... there's Padua, plain enough, that blue!
Look o'er my shoulder, follow my finger!

SEBALD
Morning?
It seems to me a night with a sun added.
Where 's dew, where 's freshness? That bruised plant, I bruised
In getting through the lattice yestereve,

Droops as it did. See, here 's my elbow's mark
I' the dust o' the sill.

OTTIMA
Oh, shut the lattice, pray!

SEBALD
Let me lean out. I cannot scent blood here,
Foul as the morn may be.
There, shut the world out!
How do you feel now, Ottima? There, curse
The world and all outside! Let us throw off
This mask: how do you bear yourself? Let 's out
With all of it!

OTTIMA
Best never speak of it.

SEBALD
Best speak again and yet again of it,
Till words cease to be more than words. "His blood,"
For instance—let those two words mean, "His blood"
And nothing more. Notice, I 'll say them now,
"His blood."

OTTIMA
Assuredly if I repented
The deed—

SEBALD
Repent? Who should repent, or why?
What puts that in your head? Did I once say
That I repented?

OTTIMA
No; I said the deed ...

SEBALD
"The deed" and "the event"—just now it was
"Our passion's fruit"—the devil take such cant!
Say, once and always, Luca was a wittol,
I am his cut-throat, you are ...

OTTIMA
Here 's the wine;
I brought it when we left the house above,
And glasses too—wine of both sorts. Black? White then?

SEBALD
But am not I his cut-throat? What are you?

OTTIMA

There trudges on his business from the Duomo
Benet the Capuchin, with his brown hood
And bare feet; always in one place at church,
Close under the stone wall by the south entry.
I used to take him for a brown cold piece
Of the wall's self, as out of it he rose
To let me pass—at first, I say, I used:
Now, so has that dumb figure fastened on me,
I rather should account the plastered wall
A piece of him, so chilly does it strike.
This, Sebald?

SEBALD

No, the white wine—the white wine!
Well, Ottima, I promised no new year
Should rise on us the ancient shameful way;
Nor does it rise. Pour on! To your black eyes!
Do you remember last damned New Year's day?

OTTIMA

You brought those foreign prints. We looked at them
Over the wine and fruit. I had to scheme
To get him from the fire. Nothing but saying
His own set wants the proof-mark, roused him up
To hunt them out.

SEBALD

'Faith, he is not alive
To fondle you before my face.

OTTIMA

Do you
Fondle me then! Who means to take your life
For that, my Sebald?

SEBALD

Hark you, Ottima!
One thing to guard against. We 'll not make much
One of the other—that is, not make more
Parade of warmth, childish officious coil,
Than yesterday: as if, sweet, I supposed
Proof upon proof were needed now, now first,
To show I love you—yes, still love you—love you
In spite of Luca and what 's come to him
—Sure sign we had him ever in our thoughts,
White sneering old reproachful face and all!
We 'll even quarrel, love, at times, as if
We still could lose each other, were not tied
By this: conceive you?

OTTIMA
Love!

SEBALD
Not tied so sure!
Because though I was wrought upon, have struck
His insolence back into him—am I
So surely yours?—therefore forever yours?

OTTIMA
Love, to be wise, (one counsel pays another,)
Should we have—months ago, when first we loved,
For instance that May morning we two stole
Under the green ascent of sycamores—
If we had come upon a thing like that
Suddenly ...

SEBALD
"A thing"—there again—"a thing!"

OTTIMA
Then, Venus' body, had we come upon
My husband Luca Gaddi's murdered corpse
Within there, at his couch-foot, covered close—
Would you have pored upon it? Why persist
In poring now upon it? For 't is here
As much as there in the deserted house:
You cannot rid your eyes of it. For me,
Now he is dead I hate him worse: I hate ...
Dare you stay here? I would go back and hold
His two dead hands, and say, "I hate you worse,
Luca, than" ...

SEBALD
Off, off—take your hands off mine,
'T is the hot evening—off! oh, morning is it?

OTTIMA
There 's one thing must be done; you know what thing.
Come in and help to carry. We may sleep
Anywhere in the whole wide house to-night.

SEBALD
What would come, think you, if we let him lie
Just as he is? Let him lie there until
The angels take him! He is turned by this
Off from his face beside, as you will see.

OTTIMA
This dusty pane might serve for looking-glass.
Three, four—four gray hairs! Is it so you said

A plait of hair should wave across my neck?
No—this way.

SEBALD
Ottima, I would give your neck,
Each splendid shoulder, both those breasts of yours,
That this were undone! Killing! Kill the world,
So Luca lives again!—ay, lives to sputter
His fulsome dotage on you—yes, and feign
Surprise that I return at eve to sup,
When all the morning I was loitering here—
Bid me dispatch my business and begone.
I would ...

OTTIMA
See!

SEBALD
No, I 'll finish. Do you think
I fear to speak the bare truth once for all?
All we have talked of, is, at bottom, fine
To suffer; there 's a recompense in guilt;
One must be venturous and fortunate:
What is one young for, else? In age we 'll sigh
O'er the wild reckless wicked days flown over;
Still, we have lived: the vice was in its place.
But to have eaten Luca's bread, have worn
His clothes, have felt his money swell my purse—
Do lovers in romances sin that way?
Why, I was starving when I used to call
And teach you music, starving while you plucked me
These flowers to smell!

OTTIMA
My poor lost friend!

SEBALD
He gave me
Life, nothing less: what if he did reproach
My perfidy, and threaten, and do more—
Had he no right? What was to wonder at?
He sat by us at table quietly:
Why must you lean across till our cheeks touched?
Could he do less than make pretence to strike?
'T is not the crime's sake—I 'd commit ten crimes
Greater, to have this crime wiped out, undone!
And you—O how feel you? Feel you for me?

OTTIMA
Well then, I love you better now than ever,
And best (look at me while I speak to you)—

Best for the crime; nor do I grieve, in truth,
This mask, this simulated ignorance,
This affectation of simplicity,
Falls off our crime; this naked crime of ours
May not now be looked over: look it down!
Great? let it be great; but the joys it brought,
Pay they or no its price? Come: they or it!
Speak not! The past, would you give up the past
Such as it is, pleasure and crime together?
Give up that noon I owned my love for you?
The garden's silence: even the single bee
Persisting in his toil, suddenly stopped,
And where he hid you only could surmise
By some campanula chalice set a-swing.
Who stammered—"Yes, I love you?"

SEBALD
And I drew
Back; put far back your face with both my hands
Lest you should grow too full of me—your face
So seemed athirst for my whole soul and body!

OTTIMA
And when I ventured to receive you here,
Made you steal hither in the mornings—

SEBALD
When
I used to look up 'neath the shrub-house here,
Till the red fire on its glazed windows spread
To a yellow haze?

OTTIMA
Ah—my sign was, the sun
Inflamed the sere side of yon chestnut-tree
Nipped by the first frost.

SEBALD
You would always laugh
At my wet boots: I had to stride through grass
Over my ankles.

OTTIMA
Then our crowning night!

SEBALD
The July night?

OTTIMA
The day of it too, Sebald!
When heaven's pillars seemed o'erbowed with heat,

Its black-blue canopy suffered descend
Close on us both, to weigh down each to each,
And smother up all life except our life.
So lay we till the storm came.

SEBALD
How it came!

OTTIMA
Buried in woods we lay, you recollect;
Swift ran the searching tempest overhead;
And ever and anon some bright white shaft
Burned through the pine-tree roof, here burned and there,
As if God's messenger through the close wood screen
Plunged and replunged his weapon at a venture,
Feeling for guilty thee and me: then broke
The thunder like a whole sea overhead—

SEBALD
Yes!

OTTIMA
—While I stretched myself upon you, hands
To hands, my mouth to your hot mouth, and shook
All my locks loose, and covered you with them—
You, Sebald, the same you!

SEBALD
Slower, Ottima!

OTTIMA
And as we lay—

SEBALD
Less vehemently! Love me!
Forgive me! Take not words, mere words, to heart!
Your breath is worse than wine. Breathe slow, speak slow!
Do not lean on me!

OTTIMA
Sebald, as we lay,
Rising and falling only with our pants,
Who said, "Let death come now! 'Tis right to die!
Right to be punished! Naught completes such bliss
But woe!" Who said that?

SEBALD
How did we ever rise?
Was 't that we slept? Why did it end?

OTTIMA

I felt you
Taper into a point the ruffled ends
Of my loose locks 'twixt both your humid lips.
My hair is fallen now: knot it again!

SEBALD
I kiss you now, dear Ottima, now and now!
This way? Will you forgive me—be once more
My great queen?

OTTIMA
Bind it thrice about my brow;
Crown me your queen, your spirit's arbitress,
Magnificent in sin. Say that!

SEBALD
I crown you
My great white queen, my spirit's arbitress,
Magnificent ...

[From without is heard the voice of **PIPPA** singing—

The year's at the spring
And day's at the morn;
Morning's at seven;
The hillside's dew-pearled;
The lark's on the wing;
The snail's on the thorn:
God's in his heaven—
All's right with the world!

[**PIPPA** passes.

SEBALD
God's in his heaven! Do you hear that? Who spoke?
You, you spoke!

OTTIMA
Oh—that little ragged girl!
She must have rested on the step: we give them
But this one holiday the whole year round.
Did you ever see our silk-mills—their inside?
There are ten silk-mills now belong to you.
She stoops to pick my double heartsease ... Sh!
She does not hear: call you out louder!

SEBALD
Leave me!
Go, get your clothes on—dress those shoulders!

OTTIMA

Sebald?

SEBALD
Wipe off that paint! I hate you.

OTTIMA
Miserable!

SEBALD
My God, and she is emptied of it now!
Outright now!—how miraculously gone
All of the grace—had she not strange grace once?
Why, the blank cheek hangs listless as it likes,
No purpose holds the features up together,
Only the cloven brow and puckered chin
Stay in their places: and the very hair,
That seemed to have a sort of life in it,
Drops, a dead web!

OTTIMA
Speak to me—not of me!

SEBALD
—That round great full-orbed face, where not an angle
Broke the delicious indolence—all broken!

OTTIMA
To me—not of me! Ungrateful, perjured cheat!
A coward too: but ingrate's worse than all!
Beggar—my slave—a fawning, cringing lie!
Leave me! Betray me! I can see your drift!
A lie that walks and eats and drinks!

SEBALD
My God!
Those morbid olive faultless shoulder-blades—
I should have known there was no blood beneath!

OTTIMA
You hate me then? You hate me then?

SEBALD
To think
She would succeed in her absurd attempt,
And fascinate by sinning, show herself
Superior—guilt from its excess superior
To innocence! That little peasant's voice
Has righted all again. Though I be lost,
I know which is the better, never fear,
Of vice or virtue, purity or lust,
Nature or trick! I see what I have done,

Entirely now! Oh I am proud to feel
Such torments—let the world take credit thence—
I, having done my deed, pay too its price!
I hate, hate—curse you! God's in his heaven!

OTTIMA
—Me!
Me! no, no, Sebald, not yourself—kill me!
Mine is the whole crime. Do but kill me—then
Yourself—then—presently—first hear me speak!
I always meant to kill myself—wait, you!
Lean on my breast—not as a breast; don't love me
The more because you lean on me, my own
Heart's Sebald! There, there, both deaths presently!

SEBALD
My brain is drowned now—quite drowned: all I feel
Is ... is, at swift-recurring intervals,
A hurry-down within me, as of waters
Loosened to smother up some ghastly pit:
There they go—whirls from a black fiery sea!

OTTIMA
Not me—to him, O God, be merciful!

[Talk by the way, while **PIPPA** is passing from the hillside to Oreana. Foreign **STUDENTS** of painting and sculpture, from Venice, assembled opposite the house of Jules, a young French statuary, at Passagno.

1st STUDENT
Attention! My own post is beneath this window, but the pomegranate clump yonder will hide three or four of you with a little squeezing, and Schramm and his pipe must lie flat in the balcony. Four, five—who's a defaulter? We want everybody, for Jules must not be suffered to hurt his bride when the jest's found out.

2nd STUDENT
All here! Only our poet's away—never having much meant to be present, moonstrike him! The airs of that fellow, that Giovacchino! He was in violent love with himself, and had a fair prospect of thriving in his suit, so unmolested was it,—when suddenly a woman falls in love with him, too; and out of pure jealousy he takes himself off to Trieste, immortal poem and all: whereto is this prophetical epitaph appended already, as Bluphocks assures me,—"Here a mammoth-poem lies, Fouled to death by butterflies." His own fault, the simpleton! Instead of cramp couplets, each like a knife in your entrails, he should write, says Bluphocks, both classically and intelligibly.—Æsculapius, an Epic. Catalogue of the drugs: Hebe's plaister—One strip Cools your lip. Phœbus' emulsion—One bottle Clears your throttle. Mercury's bolus—One box Cures ...

3rd STUDENT
Subside, my fine fellow! If the marriage was over by ten o'clock, Jules will certainly be here in a minute with his bride.

2nd STUDENT

Good!—only, so should the poet's muse have been universally acceptable, says Bluphocks, et canibus nostris ... and Delia not better known to our literary dogs than the boy Giovacchino!

1st STUDENT
To the point, now. Where's Gottlieb, the new-comer? Oh,—listen, Gottlieb, to what has called down this piece of friendly vengeance on Jules, of which we now assemble to witness the winding-up. We are all agreed, all in a tale, observe, when Jules shall burst out on us in a fury by and by: I am spokesman—the verses that are to undeceive Jules bear my name of Lutwyche—but each professes himself alike insulted by this strutting stone-squarer, who came along from Paris to Munich, and thence with a crowd of us to Venice and Possagno here, but proceeds in a day or two alone again— oh, alone indubitably!—to Rome and Florence. He, forsooth, take up his portion with these dissolute, brutalized, heartless bunglers!—so he was heard to call us all. Now, is Schramm brutalized, I should like to know? Am I heartless?

GOTTLIEB
Why, somewhat heartless; for, suppose Jules a coxcomb as much as you choose, still, for this mere coxcombry, you will have brushed off—what do folks style it?—the bloom of his life. Is it too late to alter? These love-letters now, you call his—I can't laugh at them.

4th STUDENT
Because you never read the sham letters of our inditing which drew forth these.

GOTTLIEB
His discovery of the truth will be frightful.

4th STUDENT
That's the joke. But you should have joined us at the beginning: there's no doubt he loves the girl— loves a model he might hire by the hour!

GOTTLIEB
See here! "He has been accustomed," he writes, "to have Canova's women about him, in stone, and the world's women beside him, in flesh; these being as much below, as those above, his soul's aspiration: but now he is to have the reality." There you laugh again! I say, you wipe off the very dew of his youth.

1st STUDENT
Schramm!
Take the pipe out of his mouth, somebody!
Will Jules lose the bloom of his youth?

SCHRAMM
Nothing worth keeping is ever lost in this world: look at a blossom—it drops presently, having done its service and lasted its time; but fruits succeed, and where would be the blossom's place could it continue? As well affirm that your eye is no longer in your body, because its earliest favorite, whatever it may have first loved to look on, is dead and done with—as that any affection is lost to the soul when its first object, whatever happened first to satisfy it, is superseded in due course. Keep but ever looking, whether with the body's eye or the mind's, and you will soon find something to look on! Has a man done wondering at women?—there follow men, dead and alive, to wonder at. Has he done wondering at men?—there's God to wonder at: and the faculty of wonder may be, at the same time, old and tired enough with respect to its first object, and yet young and fresh sufficiently, so far as concerns its novel one. Thus ...

1st STUDENT
Put Schramm's pipe into his mouth again! There, you see! Well, this Jules ... a wretched fribble—oh, I watched his disportings at Possagno, the other day! Canova's gallery—you know: there he marches first resolvedly past great works by the dozen without vouchsafing an eye: all at once he stops full at the Psiche-fanciulla—cannot pass that old acquaintance without a nod of encouragement—"In your new place, beauty? Then behave yourself as well here as at Munich—I see you!" Next he posts himself deliberately before the unfinished Pietà for half an hour without moving, till up he starts of a sudden, and thrusts his very nose into—I say, into—the group; by which gesture you are informed that precisely the sole point he had not fully mastered in Canova's practice was a certain method of using the drill in the articulation of the knee-joint—and that, likewise, has he mastered at length! Good-by, therefore, to poor Canova—whose gallery no longer needs detain his successor Jules, the predestinated novel thinker in marble!

5th STUDENT
Tell him about the women: go on to the women!

1st STUDENT
Why, on that matter he could never be supercilious enough. How should we be other (he said) than the poor devils you see, with those debasing habits we cherish? He was not to wallow in that mire, at least: he would wait, and love only at the proper time, and meanwhile put up with the Psiche-fanciulla. Now, I happened to hear of a young Greek—real Greek girl at Malamocco; a true Islander, do you see, with Alciphron's "hair like sea-moss"—Schramm knows!—white and quiet as an apparition, and fourteen years old at farthest,—a daughter of Natalia, so she swears—that hag Natalia, who helps us to models at three lire an hour. We selected this girl for the heroine of our jest. So first, Jules received a scented letter—somebody had seen his Tydeus at the Academy, and my picture was nothing to it: a profound admirer bade him persevere—would make herself known to him ere long. (Paolina, my little friend of the Fenice, transcribes divinely.) And in due time, the mysterious correspondent gave certain hints of her peculiar charms—the pale cheeks, the black hair—whatever, in short, had struck us in our Malamocco model: we retained her name, too— Phene, which is, by interpretation, sea-eagle. Now, think of Jules finding himself distinguished from the herd of us by such a creature! In his very first answer he proposed marrying his monitress: and fancy us over these letters, two, three times a day, to receive and dispatch! I concocted the main of it: relations were in the way—secrecy must be observed—in fine, would he wed her on trust, and only speak to her when they were indissolubly united? St—st—Here they come!

6th STUDENT
Both of them! Heaven's love, speak softly, speak within yourselves!

5th STUDENT
Look at the bridegroom! Half his hair in storm and half in calm,—patted down over the left temple,—like a frothy cup one blows on to cool it: and the same old blouse that he murders the marble in.

2nd STUDENT
Not a rich vest like yours, Hannibal Scratchy!—rich, that your face may the better set it off.

6th STUDENT
And the bride! Yes, sure enough, our Phene! Should you have known her in her clothes? How magnificently pale!

GOTTLIEB
She does not also take it for earnest, I hope?

1st STUDENT
Oh, Natalia's concern, that is! We settle with Natalia.

6th STUDENT
She does not speak—has evidently let out no word. The only thing is, will she equally remember the rest of her lesson, and repeat correctly all those verses which are to break the secret to Jules?

GOTTLIEB
How he gazes on her! Pity—pity!

1st STUDENT
They go in: now, silence! You three,—not nearer the window, mind, than that pomegranate: just where the little girl, who a few minutes ago passed us singing, is seated!

II. NOON

Over Orcana. The house of Jules, who crosses its threshold with **PHENE**: she is silent, on which **JULES** begins—

Do not die, Phene! I am yours now, you
Are mine now; let fate reach me how she likes,
If you 'll not die: so, never die! Sit here—
My work-room's single seat. I over-lean
This length of hair and lustrous front; they turn
Like an entire flower upward: eyes, lips, last
Your chin—no, last your throat turns: 't is their scent
Pulls down my face upon you. Nay, look ever
This one way till I change, grow you—I could
Change into you, beloved!

You by me,
And I by you; this is your hand in mine,
And side by side we sit: all 's true. Thank God!
I have spoken: speak you!

O my life to come!
My Tydeus must be carved that 's there in clay;
Yet how be carved, with you about the room?
Where must I place you? When I think that once
This room-full of rough block-work seemed my heaven
Without you! Shall I ever work again,
Get fairly into my old ways again,
Bid each conception stand while, trait by trait,
My hand transfers its lineaments to stone?
Will my mere fancies live near you, their truth—
The live truth, passing and repassing me,

Sitting beside me?

Now speak!

Only first,
See, all your letters! Was 't not well contrived?
Their hiding-place is Psyche's robe; she keeps
Your letters next her skin: which drops out foremost?
Ah,—this that swam down like a first moonbeam
Into my world!

Again those eyes complete
Their melancholy survey, sweet and slow,
Of all my room holds; to return and rest
On me, with pity, yet some wonder too:
As if God bade some spirit plague a world,
And this were the one moment of surprise
And sorrow while she took her station, pausing
O'er what she sees, finds good, and must destroy!
What gaze you at? Those? Books, I told you of;
Let your first word to me rejoice them, too:
This minion, a Coluthus, writ in red,
Bistre and azure by Bessarion's scribe—
Read this line ... no, shame—Homer's be the Greek
First breathed me from the lips of my Greek girl!
This Odyssey in coarse black vivid type
With faded yellow blossoms 'twixt page and page,
To mark great places with due gratitude;
"He said, and on Antinous directed
A bitter shaft" ... a flower blots out the rest!
Again upon your search? My statues, then!
—Ah, do not mind that—better that will look
When cast in bronze—an Almaign Kaiser, that,
Swart-green and gold, with truncheon based on hip.
This, rather, turn to! What, unrecognized?
I thought you would have seen that here you sit
As I imagined you,—Hippolyta,
Naked upon her bright Numidian horse.
Recall you this then? "Carve in bold relief"—
So you commanded—"carve, against I come,
A Greek, in Athens, as our fashion was,
Feasting, bay-filleted and thunder-free,
Who rises 'neath the lifted myrtle-branch.
'Praise those who slew Hipparchus!' cry the guests,
'While o'er thy head the singer's myrtle waves
As erst above our champion: stand up, all!'"
See, I have labored to express your thought.
Quite round, a cluster of mere hands and arms
(Thrust in all senses, all ways, from all sides,
Only consenting at the branch's end
They strain toward) serves for frame to a sole face,

The Praiser's, in the centre: who with eyes
Sightless, so bend they back to light inside
His brain where visionary forms throng up,
Sings, minding not that palpitating arch
Of hands and arms, nor the quick drip of wine
From the drenched leaves o'erhead, nor crowns cast off,
Violet and parsley crowns to trample on—
Sings, pausing as the patron-ghosts approve,
Devoutly their unconquerable hymn.
But you must say a "well" to that—say "well!"
Because you gaze—am I fantastic, sweet?
Gaze like my very life's-stuff, marble—marbly
Even to the silence! Why, before I found
The real flesh Phene, I inured myself
To see, throughout all nature, varied stuff
For better nature's birth by means of art:
With me, each substance tended to one form
Of beauty—to the human archetype.
On every side occurred suggestive germs
Of that—the tree, the flower—or take the fruit,—
Some rosy shape, continuing the peach,
Curved beewise o'er its bough; as rosy limbs,
Depending, nestled in the leaves; and just
From a cleft rose-peach the whole Dryad sprang.
But of the stuffs one can be master of,
How I divined their capabilities!
From the soft-rinded smoothening facile chalk
That yields your outline to the air's embrace,
Half-softened by a halo's pearly gloom;
Down to the crisp imperious steel, so sure
To cut its one confided thought clean out
Of all the world. But marble!—'neath my tools
More pliable than jelly—as it were
Some clear primordial creature dug from depths
In the earth's heart, where itself breeds itself,
And whence all baser substance may be worked;
Refine it off to air, you may,—condense it
Down to the diamond;—is not metal there,
When o'er the sudden speck my chisel trips?
—Not flesh, as flake off flake I scale, approach,
Lay bare those bluish veins of blood asleep?
Lurks flame in no strange windings where, surprised
By the swift implement sent home at once,
Flushes and glowings radiate and hover
About its track?

Phene? what—why is this?
That whitening cheek, those still dilating eyes!
Ah, you will die—I knew that you would die!

[**PHENE** begins, on his having long remained silent.

Now the end's coming; to be sure, it must
Have ended sometime! Tush, why need I speak
Their foolish speech? I cannot bring to mind
One half of it, beside; and do not care
For old Natalia now, nor any of them.
Oh, you—what are you?—if I do not try
To say the words Natalia made me learn,
To please your friends,—it is to keep myself
Where your voice lifted me, by letting that
Proceed: but can it? Even you, perhaps,
Cannot take up, now you have once let fall,
The music's life, and me along with that—
No, or you would! We'll stay, then, as we are:
Above the world.

You creature with the eyes!
If I could look forever up to them,
As now you let me,—I believe, all sin,
All memory of wrong done, suffering borne,
Would drop down, low and lower, to the earth
Whence all that's low comes, and there touch and stay
—Never to overtake the rest of me,
All that, unspotted, reaches up to you,
Drawn by those eyes! What rises is myself,
Not me the shame and suffering; but they sink,
Are left, I rise above them. Keep me so,
Above the world!

But you sink, for your eyes
Are altering—altered! Stay—"I love you, love" ...
I could prevent it if I understood:
More of your words to me: was 't in the tone
Or the words, your power?

Or stay—I will repeat
Their speech, if that contents you! Only change
No more, and I shall find it presently
Far back here, in the brain yourself filled up.
Natalia threatened me that harm should follow
Unless I spoke their lesson to the end,
But harm to me, I thought she meant, not you.
Your friends,—Natalia said they were your friends
And meant you well,—because, I doubted it,
Observing (what was very strange to see)
On every face, so different in all else,
The same smile girls like me are used to bear,
But never men, men cannot stoop so low;
Yet your friends, speaking of you, used that smile,
That hateful smirk of boundless self-conceit
Which seems to take possession of the world

And make of God a tame confederate,
Purveyor to their appetites ... you know!
But still Natalia said they were your friends,
And they assented though they smiled the more,
And all came round me,—that thin Englishman
With light lank hair seemed leader of the rest;
He held a paper—"What we want," said he,
Ending some explanation to his friends—
"Is something slow, involved and mystical,
To hold Jules long in doubt, yet take his taste
And lure him on until, at innermost
Where he seeks sweetness' soul, he may find—this!
—As in the apple's core, the noisome fly:
For insects on the rind are seen at once,
And brushed aside as soon, but this is found
Only when on the lips or loathing tongue."
And so he read what I have got by heart:
I'll speak it,—"Do not die, love! I am yours" ...
No—is not that, or like that, part of words
Yourself began by speaking? Strange to lose
What cost such pains to learn! Is this more right?

I am a painter who cannot paint;
In my life, a devil rather than saint;
In my brain, as poor a creature too:
No end to all I cannot do!
Yet do one thing at least I can—
Love a man or hate a man
Supremely: thus my lore began.
Through the Valley of Love I went,
In the lovingest spot to abide,
And just on the verge where I pitched my tent,
I found Hate dwelling beside.
(Let the Bridegroom ask what the painter meant,
Of his Bride, of the peerless Bride!)
And further, I traversed Hate's grove,
In the hatefullest nook to dwell;
But lo, where I flung myself prone, couched Love
Where the shadow threefold fell.
(The meaning—those black bride's-eyes above,
Not a painter's lip should tell!)

"And here," said he, "Jules probably will ask,
'You have black eyes, Love,—you are, sure enough,
My peerless bride,—then do you tell indeed
What needs some explanation! What means this?'"
—And I am to go on, "without a word—

So, I grew wise in Love and Hate,
From simple that I was of late.
Once, when I loved, I would enlace

Breast, eyelids, hands, feet, form and face
Of her I loved, in one embrace—
As if by mere love I could love immensely!
Once, when I hated, I would plunge
My sword, and wipe with the first lunge
My foe's whole life out like a sponge—
As if by mere hate I could hate intensely!
But now I am wiser, know better the fashion
How passion seeks aid from its opposite passion:
And if I see cause to love more, hate more
Than ever man loved, ever hated before—
And seek in the Valley of Love
The nest, or the nook in Hate's Grove
Where my soul may surely reach
The essence, naught less, of each,
The Hate of all Hates, the Love
Of all Loves, in the Valley or Grove,—
I find them the very warders
Each of the other's borders.
When I love most, Love is disguised
In Hate; and when Hate is surprised
In Love, then I hate most: ask
How Love smiles through Hate's iron casque,
Hate grins through Love's rose-braided mask,—
And how, having hated thee,
I sought long and painfully
To reach thy heart, nor prick
The skin but pierce to the quick—
Ask this, my Jules, and be answered straight
By thy bride—how the painter Lutwyche can hate!

JULES interposes.

Lutwyche! Who else? But all of them, no doubt,
Hated me: they at Venice—presently
Their turn, however! You I shall not meet:
If I dreamed, saying this would wake me.

Keep
What's here, the gold—we cannot meet again,
Consider! and the money was but meant
For two years' travel, which is over now,
All chance or hope or care or need of it.
This—and what comes from selling these, my casts
And books and medals, except ... let them go
Together, so the produce keeps you safe
Out of Natalia's clutches! If by chance
(For all's chance here) I should survive the gang
At Venice, root out all fifteen of them,
We might meet somewhere, since the world is wide.

[From without is heard the voice of **PIPPA**, singing—

Give her but a least excuse to love me!
When—where—
How—can this arm establish her above me,
If fortune fixed her as my lady there,
There already, to eternally reprove me?
("Hist!"—said Kate the Queen;
But "Oh!" cried the maiden, binding her tresses,
"'T is only a page that carols unseen,
Crumbling your hounds their messes!")

Is she wronged?—To the rescue of her honor,
My heart!
Is she poor?—What costs it to be styled a donor?
Merely an earth to cleave, a sea to part.
But that fortune should have thrust all this upon her!
("Nay, list!"—bade Kate the Queen;
And still cried the maiden, binding her tresses,
"'T is only a page that carols unseen,
Fitting your hawks their jesses!")

[**PIPPA** passes.

[**JULES** resumes.

What name was that the little girl sang forth?
Kate? The Cornaro, doubtless, who renounced
The crown of Cyprus to be lady here
At Asolo, where still her memory stays,
And peasants sing how once a certain page
Pined for the grace of her so far above
His power of doing good to, "Kate the Queen—
She never could be wronged, be poor," he sighed,
"Need him to help her!"

Yes, a bitter thing
To see our lady above all need of us;
Yet so we look ere we will love; not I,
But the world looks so. If whoever loves
Must be, in some sort, god or worshipper,
The blessing or the blest one, queen or page,
Why should we always choose the page's part?
Here is a woman with utter need of me,—
I find myself queen here, it seems!

How strange!
Look at the woman here with the new soul,
Like my own Psyche,—fresh upon her lips
Alit, the visionary butterfly,
Waiting my word to enter and make bright,

Or flutter off and leave all blank as first.
This body had no soul before, but slept
Or stirred, was beauteous or ungainly, free
From taint or foul with stain, as outward things
Fastened their image on its passiveness:
Now, it will wake, feel, live—or die again!
Shall to produce form out of unshaped stuff
Be Art—and further, to evoke a soul
From form be nothing? This new soul is mine!

Now, to kill Lutwyche, what would that do?—save
A wretched dauber, men will hoot to death
Without me, from their hooting. Oh, to hear
God's voice plain as I heard it first, before
They broke in with their laughter! I heard them
Henceforth, not God.

To Ancona—Greece—some isle!
I wanted silence only; there is clay
Everywhere. One may do whate'er one likes
In Art: the only thing is, to make sure
That one does like it—which takes pains to know.
Scatter all this, my Phene—this mad dream!
Who, what is Lutwyche, what Natalia's friends,
What the whole world except our love—my own,
Own Phene? But I told you, did I not,
Ere night we travel for your land—some isle
With the sea's silence on it? Stand aside—
I do but break these paltry models up
To begin Art afresh. Meet Lutwyche, I—
And save him from my statue meeting him?
Some unsuspected isle in the far seas!
Like a god going through his world, there stands
One mountain for a moment in the dusk,
Whole brotherhoods of cedars on its brow:
And you are ever by me while I gaze
—Are in my arms as now—as now—as now!
Some unsuspected isle in the far seas!
Some unsuspected isle in far-off seas!

[Talk by the way, while **PIPPA** is passing from Orcana to the Turret. Two or three of the Austrian
POLICE loitering with **BLUPHOCKS**, an English vagabond, just in view of the Turret.

BLUPHOCKS
So, that is your Pippa, the little girl who passed us singing? Well, your Bishop's Intendant's money
shall be honestly earned:—now, don't make me that sour face because I bring the Bishop's name
into the business; we know he can have nothing to do with such horrors: we know that he is a saint
and all that a bishop should be, who is a great man beside. Oh were but every worm a maggot, Every
fly a grig, Every bough a Christmas fagot, Every tune a jig! In fact, I have abjured all religions; but the
last I inclined to was the Armenian: for I have travelled, do you see, and at Koenigsberg, Prussia
Improper (so styled because there's a sort of bleak hungry sun there), you might remark, over a

venerable house-porch, a certain Chaldee inscription; and brief as it is, a mere glance at it used absolutely to change the mood of every bearded passenger. In they turned, one and all; the young and lightsome, with no irreverent pause, the aged and decrepit, with a sensible alacrity: 't was the Grand Rabbi's abode, in short. Struck with curiosity, I lost no time in learning Syriac—(these are vowels, you dogs,—follow my stick's end in the mud—Celarent, Darii, Ferio!) and one morning presented myself, spelling-book in hand, a, b, c,—I picked it out letter by letter, and what was the purport of this miraculous posy? Some cherished legend of the past, you'll say—"How Moses hocus-pocussed Egypt's land with fly and locust,"—or, "How to Jonah sounded harshish, Get thee up and go to Tarshish,"—or "How the angel meeting Balaam, Straight his ass returned a salaam." In no wise! "Shackabrack—Boach—somebody or other—Isaach, Re-cei-ver, Pur-cha-ser and Ex-chan-ger of—Stolen Goods!" So, talk to me of the religion of a bishop! I have renounced all bishops save Bishop Beveridge!—mean to live so—and die—As some Greek dog-sage, dead and merry, Hellward bound in Charon's wherry, With food for both worlds, under and upper, Lupine-seed and Hecate's supper, And never an obolus ... (though thanks to you, or this Intendant through you, or this Bishop through his Intendant—I possess a burning pocket-full of zwanzigers) ... To pay the Stygian Ferry!

1st POLICEMAN
There is the girl, then; go and deserve them the moment you have pointed out to us Signor Luigi and his mother. [To the **REST**] I have been noticing a house yonder, this long while: not a shutter unclosed since morning!

2nd POLICEMAN
Old Luca Gaddi's, that owns the silk-mills here: he dozes by the hour, wakes up, sighs deeply, says he should like to be Prince Metternich, and then dozes again, after having bidden young Sebald, the foreigner, set his wife to playing draughts. Never molest such a household, they mean well.

BLUPHOCKS
Only, cannot you tell me something of this little Pippa, I must have to do with? One could make something of that name. Pippa—that is, short for Felippa—rhyming to Panurge consults Hertrippa—Believest thou, King Agrippa? Something might be done with that name.

2nd POLICEMAN
Put into rhyme that your head and a ripe muskmelon would not be dear at half a zwanziger! Leave this fooling, and look out; the afternoon's over or nearly so.

3rd POLICEMAN
Where in this passport of Signor Luigi does our Principal instruct you to watch him so narrowly? There? What's there beside a simple signature? (That English fool's busy watching.)

2nd POLICEMAN
Flourish all round—"Put all possible obstacles in his way;" oblong dot at the end—"Detain him till further advices reach you;" scratch at bottom—"Send him back on pretence of some informality in the above;" ink-spirt on righthand side (which is the case here)—"Arrest him at once." Why and wherefore, I don't concern myself, but my instructions amount to this: if Signor Luigi leaves home to-night for Vienna—well and good, the passport deposed with us for our visa is really for his own use, they have misinformed the Office, and he means well; but let him stay over to-night—there has been the pretence we suspect, the accounts of his corresponding and holding intelligence with the Carbonari are correct, we arrest him at once, to-morrow comes Venice, and presently Spielberg. Bluphocks makes the signal, sure enough! That is he, entering the turret with his mother, no doubt.

Inside the Turret on the Hill above Asolo. **LUIGI** and his **MOTHER** entering.

MOTHER
If there blew wind, you'd hear a long sigh, easing
The utmost heaviness of music's heart.

LUIGI
. Here in the archway?

MOTHER
Oh no, no—in farther,
Where the echo is made, on the ridge.

LUIGI
Here surely, then.
How plain the tap of my heel as I leaped up!
Hark—"Lucius Junius!" The very ghost of a voice
Whose body is caught and kept by ... what are those?
Mere withered wallflowers, waving overhead?
They seem an elvish group with thin bleached hair
That lean out of their topmost fortress—look
And listen, mountain men, to what we say,
Hand under chin of each grave earthy face.
Up and show faces all of you!—"All of you!"
That 's the king dwarf with the scarlet comb; old Franz,
Come down and meet your fate? Hark—"Meet your fate!"

MOTHER
Let him not meet it, my Luigi—do not
Go to his City! Putting crime aside,
Half of these ills of Italy are feigned:
Your Pellicos and writers for effect,
Write for effect.

LUIGI
Hush! Say A writes, and B.

MOTHER
These A's and B's write for effect, I say.
Then, evil is in its nature loud, while good
Is silent; you hear each petty injury,
None of his virtues; he is old beside,
Quiet and kind, and densely stupid. Why
Do A and B kill not him themselves?

LUIGI
They teach
Others to kill him—me—and, if I fail,

Others to succeed; now, if A tried and failed,
I could not teach that: mine 's the lesser task.
Mother, they visit night by night ...

MOTHER
—You, Luigi?
Ah, will you let me tell you what you are?

LUIGI
Why not? Oh, the one thing you fear to hint,
You may assure yourself I say and say
Ever to myself! At times—nay, even as now
We sit—I think my mind is touched, suspect
All is not sound: but is not knowing that,
What constitutes one sane or otherwise?
I know I am thus—so, all is right again.
I laugh at myself as through the town I walk,
And see men merry as if no Italy
Were suffering; then I ponder—"I am rich,
Young, healthy; why should this fact trouble me,
More than it troubles these?" But it does trouble.
No, trouble 's a bad word: for as I walk
There 's springing and melody and giddiness,
And old quaint turns and passages of my youth,
Dreams long forgotten, little in themselves,
Return to me—whatever may amuse me:
And earth seems in a truce with me, and heaven
Accords with me, all things suspend their strife,
The very cicala laughs "There goes he, and there!
Feast him, the time is short; he is on his way
For the world's sake: feast him this once, our friend!"
And in return for all this, I can trip
Cheerfully up the scaffold-steps. I go
This evening, mother!

MOTHER
But mistrust yourself—
Mistrust the judgment you pronounce on him!

LUIGI
Oh, there I feel—am sure that I am right!

MOTHER
Mistrust your judgment then, of the mere means
To this wild enterprise: say, you are right,—
How should one in your state e'er bring to pass
What would require a cool head, a cool heart,
And a calm hand? You never will escape.

LUIGI
Escape? To even wish that, would spoil all.

The dying is best part of it. Too much
Have I enjoyed these fifteen years of mine,
To leave myself excuse for longer life:
Was not life pressed down, running o'er with joy,
That I might finish with it ere my fellows
Who, sparelier feasted, make a longer stay?
I was put at the board-head, helped to all
At first; I rise up happy and content.
God must be glad one loves his world so much.
I can give news of earth to all the dead
Who ask me:—last year's sunsets, and great stars
Which had a right to come first and see ebb
The crimson wave that drifts the sun away—
Those crescent moons with notched and burning rims
That strengthened into sharp fire, and there stood,
Impatient of the azure—and that day
In March, a double rainbow stopped the storm—
May's warm slow yellow moonlit summer nights—
Gone are they, but I have them in my soul!

MOTHER
He will not go!

LUIGI
You smile at me? 'T is true,—
Voluptuousness, grotesqueness, ghastliness,
Environ my devotedness as quaintly
As round about some antique altar wreathe
The rose festoons, goats' horns, and oxen's skulls.

MOTHER
See now: you reach the city, you must cross
His threshold—how?

LUIGI
Oh, that's if we conspired!
Then would come pains in plenty, as you guess—
But guess not how the qualities most fit
For such an office, qualities I have,
Would little stead me, otherwise employed,
Yet prove of rarest merit only here.
Every one knows for what his excellence
Will serve, but no one ever will consider
For what his worst defect might serve: and yet
Have you not seen me range our coppice yonder
In search of a distorted ash?—I find
The wry spoilt branch a natural perfect bow.
Fancy the thrice-sage, thrice-precautioned man
Arriving-at the palace on my errand!
No, no! I have a handsome dress packed up—
White satin here, to set off my black hair;

In I shall march—for you may watch your life out
Behind thick walls, make friends there to betray you;
More than one man spoils everything. March straight—
Only, no clumsy knife to fumble for,
Take the great gate, and walk (not saunter) on
Through guards and guards— I have rehearsed it all
Inside the turret here a hundred times.
Don't ask the way of whom you meet, observe!
But where they cluster thickliest is the door
Of doors; they'll let you pass—they'll never blab
Each to the other, he knows not the favorite,
Whence he is bound and what's his business now.
Walk in—straight up to him; you have no knife:
Be prompt, how should he scream? Then, out with you!
Italy, Italy, my Italy!
You 're free, you 're free! Oh mother, I could dream
They got about me—Andrea from his exile,
Pier from his dungeon, Gualtier from his grave!

MOTHER
Well, you shall go. Yet seems this patriotism
The easiest virtue for a selfish man
To acquire: he loves himself,—and next, the world—
If he must love beyond,—but naught between:
As a short-sighted man sees naught midway
His body and the sun above. But you
Are my adored Luigi, ever obedient
To my least wish, and running o'er with love:
I could not call you cruel or unkind.
Once more, your ground for killing him!—then go!

LUIGI
Now do you try me, or make sport of me?
How first the Austrians got these provinces ...
(If that is all, I 'll satisfy you soon)
—Never by conquest but by cunning, for
That treaty whereby ...

MOTHER
Well?

LUIGI
Sure, he 's arrived,
The tell-tale cuckoo: spring 's his confidant,
And he lets out her April purposes!
Or ... better go at once to modern time.
He has ... they have ... in fact, I understand
But can't restate the matter; that's my boast:
Others could reason it out to you, and prove
Things they have made me feel.

MOTHER

Why go to-night?
Morn 's for adventure. Jupiter is now
A morning-star. I cannot hear you, Luigi!

LUIGI

"I am the bright and morning-star," saith God—
And, "to such an one I give the morning-star."
The gift of the morning-star! Have I God's gift
Of the morning-star?

MOTHER

Chiara will love to see
That Jupiter an evening-star next June.

LUIGI

True, mother. Well for those who live through June!
Great noontides, thunder-storms, all glaring pomps
That triumph at the heels of June the god
Leading his revel through our leafy world.
Yes, Chiara will be here.

MOTHER

In June: remember,
Yourself appointed that month for her coming.

LUIGI

Was that low noise the echo?

MOTHER

The night-wind.
She must be grown—with her blue eyes upturned
As if life were one long and sweet surprise:
In June she comes.

LUIGI

We were to see together
The Titian at Treviso. There, again!

[From without is heard the voice of **PIPPA**, singing—

A king lived long ago,
In the morning of the world,
When earth was nigher heaven than now;
And the king's locks curled,
Disparting o'er a forehead full
As the milk-white space 'twixt horn and horn
Of some sacrificial bull—
Only calm as a babe new-born:
For he was got to a sleepy mood,
So safe from all decrepitude,

Age with its bane, so sure gone by,
(The gods so loved him while he dreamed)
That, having lived thus long, there seemed
No need the king should ever die.

LUIGI
No need that sort of king should ever die!

Among the rocks his city was:
Before his palace, in the sun,
He sat to see his people pass,
And judge them every one
From its threshold of smooth stone.
They haled him many a valley-thief
Caught in the sheep-pens, robber-chief
Swarthy and shameless, beggar-cheat,
Spy-prowler, or rough pirate found
On the sea-sand left aground;
And sometimes clung about his feet,
With bleeding lip and burning cheek,
A woman, bitterest wrong to speak
Of one with sullen thickset brows:
And sometimes from the prison-house
The angry priests a pale wretch brought,
Who through some chink had pushed and pressed
On knees and elbows, belly and breast,
Worm-like into the temple,—caught
He was by the very god,
Who ever in the darkness strode
Backward and forward, keeping watch
O'er his brazen bowls, such rogues to catch!
These, all and every one,
The king judged, sitting in the sun.

LUIGI
That king should still judge sitting in the sun!

His councillors, on left and right,
Looked anxious up,—but no surprise
Disturbed the king's old smiling eyes
Where the very blue had turned to white.
'Tis said, a Python scared one day
The breathless city, till he came,
With forky tongue and eyes on flame.
Where the old king sat to judge alway;
But when he saw the sweepy hair
Girt with a crown of berries rare
Which the god will hardly give to wear
To the maiden who singeth, dancing bare
In the altar-smoke by the pine-torch lights,
At his wondrous forest rites,—

Seeing this, he did not dare
Approach that threshold in the sun,
Assault the old king smiling there.
Such grace had kings when the world begun!

[**PIPPA** passes.

LUIGI
And such grace have they, now that the world ends!
The Python at the city, on the throne,
And brave men, God would crown for slaying him,
Lurk in by-corners lest they fall his prey.
Are crowns yet to be won in this late time,
Which weakness makes me hesitate to reach?
'T is God's voice calls: how could I stay? Farewell!

[Talk by the way, while **PIPPA** is passing from the Turret to the Bishop's Brother's House, close to the Duomo S. Maria. Poor **GIRLS** sitting on the steps.

1st GIRL
There goes a swallow to Venice—the stout seafarer!
Seeing those birds fly, makes one wish for wings.
Let us all wish; you, wish first!

2nd GIRL
I? This sunset
To finish.

3rd GIRL
That old—somebody I know,
Grayer and older than my grandfather,
To give me the same treat he gave last week—
Feeding me on his knee with fig-peckers,
Lampreys and red Breganze-wine, and mumbling
The while some folly about how well I fare,
Let sit and eat my supper quietly:
Since had he not himself been late this morning
Detained at—never mind where,—had he not ...
"Eh, baggage, had I not!"—

2nd GIRL
How she can lie!

3rd GIRL
Look there—by the nails!

2nd GIRL
What makes your fingers red?

3rd GIRL
Dipping them into wine to write bad words with

On the bright table: how he laughed!

1st GIRL
My turn.
Spring's come and summer's coming. I would wear
A long loose gown, down to the feet and hands,
With plaits here, close about the throat, all day;
And all night lie, the cool long nights, in bed;
And have new milk to drink, apples to eat,
Deuzans and junetings, leather-coats ... ah, I should say,
This is away in the fields—miles!

3rd GIRL
Say at once
You'd be at home: she'd always be at home!
Now comes the story of the farm among
The cherry orchards, and how April snowed
White blossoms on her as she ran. Why, fool,
They've rubbed the chalk-mark out, how tall you were,
Twisted your starling's neck, broken his cage,
Made a dung-hill of your garden!

1st GIRL
They destroy
My garden since I left them? well—perhaps
I would have done so: so I hope they have!
A fig-tree curled out of our cottage wall;
They called it mine, I have forgotten why,
It must have been there long ere I was born:
Cric—cric—I think I hear the wasps o'erhead
Pricking the papers strung to flutter there
And keep off birds in fruit-time—coarse long papers,
And the wasps eat them, prick them through and through.

3rd GIRL
How her month twitches! Where was I?—before
She broke in with her wishes and long gowns
And wasps—would I be such a fool!—Oh, here!
This is my way: I answer every one
Who asks me why I make so much of him—
(If you say, "you love him"—straight "he 'll not be gulled!")
"He that seduced me when I was a girl
Thus high—had eyes like yours, or hair like yours,
Brown, red, white,"—as the case may be: that pleases!
See how that beetle burnishes in the path!
There sparkles he along the dust: and, there—
Your journey to that maize-tuft spoiled; at least!

1st GIRL
When I was young, they said if you killed one
Of those sunshiny beetles, that his friend

Up there, would shine no more that day nor next.

2nd GIRL
When you were young? Nor are you young, that's true.
How your plump arms, that were, have dropped away!
Why, I can span them. Cecco beats you still?
No matter, so you keep your curious hair.
I wish they'd find a way to dye our hair
Your color—any lighter tint, indeed,
Than black: the men say they are sick of black,
Black eyes, black hair!

4th GIRL
Sick of yours, like enough.
Do you pretend you ever tasted lampreys
And ortolans? Giovita, of the palace,
Engaged (but there's no trusting him) to slice me
Polenta with a knife that had cut up
An ortolan.

2nd GIRL
Why, there! Is not that Pippa
We are to talk to, under the window,—quick!—
Where the lights are?

1st GIRL
That she? No, or she would sing,
For the Intendant said ...

3d GIRL
Oh, you sing first!
Then, if she listens and comes close ... I'll tell you,—
Sing that song the young English noble made,
Who took you for the purest of the pure,
And meant to leave the world for you—what fun!

2nd GIRL [Sings]
You'll love me yet!—and I can tarry
Your love's protracted growing:
June reared that bunch of flowers you carry,
From seeds of April's sowing.

I plant a heartfull now: some seed
At least is sure to strike,
And yield—what you'll not pluck indeed,
Not love, but, may be, like.

You'll look at least on love's remains,
A grave's one violet:
Your look?—that pays a thousand pains.
What's death? You'll love me yet!

3rd GIRL [To **PIPPA** who approaches]

Oh, you may come closer—we shall not eat you! Why, you seem the very person that the great rich handsome Englishman has fallen so violently in love with. I 'll tell you all about it.

IV. NIGHT

Inside the Palace by the Duomo. **MONSIGNOR**, dismissing his **ATTENDANTS**.

MONSIGNOR

Thanks, friends, many thanks! I chiefly desire life now, that I may recompense every one of you. Most I know something of already. What, a repast prepared? Benedicto benedicatur ... ugh, ugh! Where was I? Oh, as you were remarking, Ugo, the weather is mild, very unlike winter-weather: but I am a Sicilian, you know, and shiver in your Julys here. To be sure, when 'twas full summer at Messina, as we priests used to cross in procession the great square on Assumption Day, you might see our thickest yellow tapers twist suddenly in two, each like a falling star, or sink down on themselves in a gore of wax. But go, my friends, but go! [To the **INTENDANT**] Not you, Ugo!

[The others leave the apartment.

I have long wanted to converse with you, Ugo.

INTENDANT

Uguccio—

MONSIGNOR

... 'guccio Stefani, man! of Ascoli, Fermo and Fossombruno;—what I do need instructing about, are these accounts of your administration of my poor brother's affairs. Ugh! I shall never get through a third part of your accounts; take some of these dainties before we attempt it, however. Are you bashful to that degree? For me, a crust and water suffice.

INTENDANT

Do you choose this especial night to question me?

MONSIGNOR

This night, Ugo. You have managed my late brother's affairs since the death of our elder brother: fourteen years and a month, all but three days. On the Third of December, I find him ...

INTENDANT

If you have so intimate an acquaintance with your brother's affairs, you will be tender of turning so far back: they will hardly bear looking into, so far back.

MONSIGNOR

Ay, ay, ugh, ugh,—nothing but disappointments here below! I remark a considerable payment made to yourself on this Third of December. Talk of disappointments! There was a young fellow here, Jules, a foreign sculptor I did my utmost to advance, that the Church might be a gainer by us both: he was going on hopefully enough, and of a sudden he notifies to me some marvellous change that has happened in his notions of Art. Here's his letter,—"He never had a clearly conceived Ideal within his brain till to-day. Yet since his hand could manage a chisel, he has practised expressing other men's Ideals; and, in the very perfection he has attained to, he foresees an ultimate failure: his unconscious hand will pursue its prescribed course of old years, and will reproduce with a fatal expertness the ancient types, let the novel one appear never so palpably to his spirit. There is but one method of escape: confiding the virgin type to as chaste a hand, he will turn painter instead of sculptor, and paint, not carve, its characteristics,"—strike out, I dare say, a school like Correggio: how think you, Ugo?

INTENDANT
Is Correggio a painter?

MONSIGNOR
Foolish Jules! and yet, after all, why foolish? He may—probably will—fail egregiously; but if there should arise a new painter, will it not be in some such way, by a poet now, or a musician (spirits who have conceived and perfected an Ideal through some other channel), transferring it to this, and escaping our conventional roads by pure ignorance of them; eh, Ugo? If you have no appetite, talk at least, Ugo!

INTENDANT
Sir, I can submit no longer to this course of yours. First, you select the group of which I formed one,—next you thin it gradually,—always retaining me with your smile,—and so do you proceed till you have fairly got me alone with you between four stone walls. And now then? Let this farce, this chatter end now: what is it you want with me?

MONSIGNOR
Ugo!

INTENDANT
From the instant you arrived, I felt your smile on me as you questioned me about this and the other article in those papers—why your brother should have given me this villa, that podere,—and your nod at the end meant,—what?

MONSIGNOR
Possibly that I wished for no loud talk here. If once you set me coughing, Ugo!—

INTENDANT
I have your brother's hand and seal to all I possess: now ask me what for! what service I did him—ask me!

MONSIGNOR
I would better not: I should rip up old disgraces, let out my poor brother's weaknesses. By the way, Maffeo of Forli, (which, I forgot to observe, is your true name,) was the interdict ever taken off you for robbing that church at Cesena?

INTENDANT
No, nor needs be: for when I murdered your brother's friend, Pasquale, for him ...

MONSIGNOR
Ah, he employed you in that business, did he? Well, I must let you keep, as you say, this villa and that podere, for fear the world should find out my relations were of so indifferent a stamp? Maffeo, my family is the oldest in Messina, and century after century have my progenitors gone on polluting themselves with every wickedness under heaven: my own father ... rest his soul!—I have, I know, a

chapel to support that it may rest: my dear two dead brothers were,—what you know tolerably well; I, the youngest, might have rivalled them in vice, if not in wealth: but from my boyhood I came out from among them, and so am not partaker of their plagues. My glory springs from another source; or if from this, by contrast only,—for I, the bishop, am the brother of your employers, Ugo. I hope to repair some of their wrong, however; so far as my brother's ill-gotten treasure reverts to me, I can stop the consequences of his crime: and not one soldo shall escape me. Maffeo, the sword we quiet men spurn away, you shrewd knaves pick up and commit murders with; what opportunities the virtuous forego, the villanous seize. Because, to pleasure myself apart from other considerations, my food would be millet-cake, my dress sackcloth, and my couch straw,—am I therefore to let you, the off-scouring-of the earth, seduce the poor and ignorant by appropriating a pomp these will be sure to think lessens the abominations so unaccountably and exclusively associated with it? Must I let villas and poderi go to you, a murderer and thief, that you may beget by means of them other murderers and thieves? No—if my cough would but allow me to speak!

INTENDANT
What am I to expect? You are going to punish me?

MONSIGNOR
Must punish you, Maffeo. I cannot afford to cast away a chance. I have whole centuries of sin to redeem, and only a month or two of life to do it in. How should I dare to say ...

INTENDANT
"Forgive us our trespasses"?

MONSIGNOR
My friend, it is because I avow myself a very worm, sinful beyond measure, that I reject a line of conduct you would applaud perhaps. Shall I proceed, as it were, a-pardoning?—I?—who have no symptom of reason to assume that aught less than my strenuousest efforts will keep myself out of mortal sin, much less keep others out. No: I do trespass, but will not double that by allowing you to trespass.

INTENDANT
And suppose the villas are not your brother's to give, nor yours to take? Oh, you are hasty enough just now!

MONSIGNOR
1, 2—N°. 3!—ay, can you read the substance of a letter, N°. 3, I have received from Rome? It is precisely on the ground there mentioned, of the suspicion I have that a certain child of my late elder brother, who would have succeeded to his estates, was murdered in infancy by you, Maffeo, at the instigation of my late younger brother—that the Pontiff enjoins on me not merely the bringing that Maffeo to condign punishment, but the taking all pains, as guardian of the infant's heritage for the Church, to recover it parcel by parcel, howsoever, whensoever, and wheresoever. While you are now gnawing those fingers, the police are engaged in sealing up your papers, Maffeo, and the mere raising my voice brings my people from the next room to dispose of yourself. But I want you to confess quietly, and save me raising my voice. Why, man, do I not know the old story? The heir between the succeeding heir, and this heir's ruffianly instrument, and their complot's effect, and the life of fear and bribes and ominous smiling silence? Did you throttle or stab my brother's infant? Come now!

INTENDANT

So old a story, and tell it no better? When did such an instrument ever produce such an effect? Either the child smiles in his face; or, most likely, he is not fool enough to put himself in the employer's power so thoroughly: the child is always ready to produce—as you say—howsoever, wheresoever, and whensoever.

MONSIGNOR
Liar!

INTENDANT
Strike me? Ah, so might a father chastise! I shall sleep soundly to-night at least, though the gallows await me to-morrow; for what a life did I lead! Carlo of Cesena reminds me of his connivance, every time I pay his annuity; which happens commonly thrice a year. If I remonstrate, he will confess all to the good bishop—you!

MONSIGNOR
I see through the trick, caitiff! I would you spoke truth for once. All shall be sifted, however—seven times sifted.

INTENDANT
And how my absurd riches encumbered me! I dared not lay claim to above half my possessions. Let me but once unbosom myself, glorify Heaven, and die!

Sir, you are no brutal dastardly idiot like your brother I frightened to death: let us understand one another. Sir, I will make away with her for you—the girl—here close at hand; not the stupid obvious kind of killing; do not speak—know nothing of her nor of me! I see her every day—saw her this morning: of course there is to be no killing; but at Rome the courtesans perish off every three years, and I can entice her thither—have indeed begun operations already. There's a certain lusty blue-eyed florid-complexioned English knave, I and the Police employ occasionally. You assent, I perceive—no, that's not it—assent I do not say—but you will let me convert my present havings and holdings into cash, and give me time to cross the Alps? 'Tis but a little black-eyed pretty singing Felippa, gay silk-winding girl. I have kept her out of harm's way up to this present; for I always intended to make your life a plague to you with her. 'T is as well settled once and forever. Some women I have procured will pass Bluphocks, my handsome scoundrel, off for somebody; and once Pippa entangled!—you conceive? Through her singing? Is it a bargain?

[From without is heard the voice of **PIPPA**, singing—

Overhead the tree-tops meet,
Flowers and grass spring 'neath one's feet;
There was naught above me, naught below,
My childhood had not learned to know:
For, what are the voices of birds
—Ay, and of beasts,—but words, our words,
Only so much more sweet?
The knowledge of that with my life begun.
But I had so near made out the sun,
And counted your stars, the seven and one,
Like the fingers of my hand:
Nay, I could all but understand
Wherefore through heaven the white moon ranges;
And just when out of her soft fifty changes

No unfamiliar face might overlook me—
Suddenly God took me.

[**PIPPA** passes.

MONSIGNOR [Springing up]
My people—one and all—all—within there! Gag this villain—tie him hand and foot! He dares ... I
know not half he dares—but remove him—quick! Miserere mei, Domine! Quick, I say!

[**PIPPA'S** Chamber again. She enters it.

The bee with his comb,
The mouse at her dray,
The grub in his tomb,
While winter away;
But the fire-fly and hedge-shrew and lob-worm, I pray,
How fare they?
Ha, ha, thanks for your counsel, my Zanze!
"Feast upon lampreys, quaff Breganze"—
The summer of life so easy to spend,
And care for to-morrow so soon put away!
But winter hastens at summer's end,
And fire-fly, hedge-shrew, lob-worm, pray,
How fare they?
No bidding me then to ... what did Zanze say?
"Pare your nails pearlwise, get your small feet shoes
More like" ... (what said she?)—"and less like canoes!"
How pert that girl was!—would I be those pert
Impudent staring women! It had done me,
However, surely no such mighty hurt
To learn his name who passed that jest upon me:
No foreigner, that I can recollect,
Came, as she says, a month since, to inspect
Our silk-mills—none with blue eyes and thick rings
Of raw-silk-colored hair, at all events.
Well, if old Luca keep his good intents,
We shall do better, see what next year brings!
I may buy shoes, my Zanze, not appear
More destitute than you perhaps next year!
Bluph ... something! I had caught the uncouth name
But for Monsignor's people's sudden clatter
Above us—bound to spoil such idle chatter
As ours: it were indeed a serious matter
If silly talk like ours should put to shame
The pious man, the man devoid of blame,
The ... ah but—ah but, all the same,
No mere mortal has a right
To carry that exalted air;
Best people are not angels quite:
While—not the worst of people's doings scare
The devil; so there 's that proud look to spare!

Which is mere counsel to myself, mind! for
I have just been the holy Monsignor:
And I was you too, Luigi's gentle mother,
And you too, Luigi!—how that Luigi started
Out of the turret—doubtlessly departed
On some good errand or another,
For he passed just now in a traveller's trim,
And the sullen company that prowled
About his path, I noticed, scowled
As if they had lost a prey in him.
And I was Jules the sculptor's bride,
And I was Ottima beside,
And now what am I?—tired of fooling.
Day for folly, night for schooling!
New year's day is over and spent,
Ill or well, I must be content.
Even my lily 's asleep, I vow:
Wake up—here 's a friend I've plucked you!
Call this flower a heart's-ease now!
Something rare, let me instruct you,
Is this, with petals triply swollen,
Three times spotted, thrice the pollen;
While the leaves and parts that witness
Old proportions and their fitness,
Here remain unchanged, unmoved now;
Call this pampered thing improved now!
Suppose there 's a king of the flowers
And a girl-show held in his bowers—
"Look ye, buds, this growth of ours,"
Says he, "Zanze from the Brenta,
I have made her gorge polenta
Till both cheeks are near as bouncing
As her ... name there 's no pronouncing!
See this heightened color too,
For she swilled Breganze wine
Till her nose turned deep carmine;
'T was but white when wild she grew.
And only by this Zanze's eyes
Of which we could not change the size,
The magnitude of all achieved
Otherwise, may be perceived."

Oh what a drear dark close to my poor day!
How could that red sun drop in that black cloud?
Ah Pippa, morning's rule is moved away,
Dispensed with, never more to be allowed!
Day's turn is over, now arrives the night's.
Oh lark, be day's apostle
To mavis, merle and throstle,
Bid them their betters jostle
From day and its delights!

But at night, brother owlet, over the woods,
Toll the world to thy chantry;
Sing to the bats' sleek sisterhoods
Full complines with gallantry:
Then, owls and bats,
Cowls and twats,
Monks and nuns, in a cloister's moods,
Adjourn to the oak-stump pantry!

[After she has begun to undress herself.

Now, one thing I should like to really know:
How near I ever might approach all these
I only fancied being, this long day:
—Approach, I mean, so as to touch them, so
As to ... in some way ... move them—if you please,
Do good or evil to them some slight way.
For instance, if I wind
Silk to-morrow, my silk may bind

[Sitting on the bedside.

And border Ottima's cloak's hem.
Ah me, and my important part with them,
This morning's hymn half promised when I rose!
True in some sense or other, I suppose.

[As she lies down.

God bless me! I can pray no more to-night.
No doubt, some way or other, hymns say right.

All service ranks the same with God—
With God, whose puppets, best and worst,
Are we; there is no last nor first.

[She sleeps.

Robert Browning – A Short Biography

He is the equal of any Victorian Poet that could be mentioned. However, Browning continues to be in the shadow of Tennyson, Arnold, Hopkins, Morris and many others.

Robert Browning was born on May 7th, 1812 in Walworth in the parish of Camberwell, London. He was baptized on June 14th, 1812, at Lock's Fields Independent Chapel, York Street, Walworth.

Browning's early years were certainly very interesting. His mother was an excellent pianist and a very devout evangelical Christian. His father, who worked as a clerk at the Bank of England, was also an artist, scholar, antiquarian, and collector of books and pictures. Indeed, he amassed more than

6,000 volumes of rare books including works in Greek, Hebrew, Latin, French, Italian, and Spanish. For the young and curious Browning, it was a wonderful resource, added to which his father was a guiding force in his education.

Many accounts attest that Browning was already proficient at reading and writing by the age of five. He is said to have been a bright but anxious student and to have studied and learnt Latin, Greek, and French by the time he was fourteen. From fourteen to sixteen he was educated at home, tutored in music, drawing, dancing, and horsemanship. Certainly, language and the arts were two areas the young Browning both absorbed and pushed himself towards.

At the age of twelve he wrote a volume of Byronic verse he called Incondita, which his parents attempted to have published. The attempts were unsuccessful and, disappointed, Browning destroyed the work.

In 1825, a cousin gave Browning a collection of Percy Bysshe Shelley's poetry; Browning was so enamored with the poems that he asked for the rest of Shelley's works for his thirteenth birthday. In fact, Browning then went the extra mile, declaring himself to be both a vegetarian and an atheist in honour of his hero.

Intriguingly it seems that the rejection of his first volume didn't dim his appreciation of other poets, but it appears to have stopped him writing any poems between the ages of thirteen and twenty.

In 1828, Browning enrolled at the newly-opened University of London. He was uncomfortable with the experience and he soon left, anxious to read and absorb at his own pace.

His education which, overall is notably rambling and lacks a structure that many of his artistic contemporaries enjoyed, i.e. excellent public schooling and then a degree at Oxford or Cambridge, may present many of his critics with ammunition to criticize, but alternatively his hap-hazard education certainly contributed to many of the references that baffled both critics and his audience, but they tellingly show the breath and scale of what he could turn words too. What others would call obscure references were, to Browning, remarkably obvious.

Browning's early career was very promising. His long poem Pauline (of which only a fragment was ever finished and published) brought him to the attention of the Pre-Raphaelite master Dante Gabriel Rossetti and his difficult Paracelsus (published in 1835) was warmly admired by both Dickens and Wordsworth.

In the 1830s he met the actor William Macready and was encouraged to develop and turn his talents to the stage by writing verse drama. But these plays, including Strafford, which ran for five nights in 1837, and those contained within the Bells and Pomegranates series, were, for the most part, unsuccessful.

During this period Browning began to discover that his real talents lay in taking a single character and allowing that character to discover more about himself by revealing further personal aspects of himself in his speeches; the dramatic monologue. The techniques he developed through this—especially the use of diction, rhythm, and symbol—are regarded as his most important contribution to poetry. They would later influence such major poets of the 20th Century as Ezra Pound, T. S. Eliot, and Robert Frost.

By 1840, with the publication of Sordello, the tide turned somewhat. Many thought he was being deliberately obscure, opaque beyond measure and his poetry for the next decade or so was not eagerly acquired or talked about.

As Browning attempted to rehabilitate his career he began a relationship with Elizabeth Barrett in 1845. He had read her poems and, being totally charmed by their quality, was determined to meet her. The poetess was better known than the younger Browning but suffered from a debilitating illness and was also subject to the harsh behaviour of her over-bearing father. Nevertheless, the new couple were soon inseparable.

Her father, as he did with any of his children that married, disinherited her. Despite this she had some money from her own resources and sensing that the best outcome for both the relationship and her own health was to move abroad the couple did just that. After a private marriage at St Marylebone Parish Church, in September 1846, they journeyed to Europe to honeymoon in Paris.

Their new life now took them to Italy, first to Pisa and a little later to Florence. There they absorbed life and one another.

But in the short term the literary assault on Browning's work did not let up. He was now criticized by such patrician writers as Charles Kingsley for his abandonment of England for foreign lands. Browning could do little to answer these attacks except to compose with his pen and continue with his poetical journey.

The Browning's were well respected, and even famous. Elizabeth health began to improve, she grew stronger and in 1849, at the age of 43, between four miscarriages, she gave birth to a son, Robert Wiedeman Barrett Browning, whom they nicknamed "Penini" or "Pen",

Intriguingly despite his growing reputation and return to form as a poet he was more often than not known as 'Elizabeth Barrett's husband'.

Work flowed from his pen that was to ensure his reputation as one of England's leading poets. When his collection Men and Women was published in 1855 it contained some of his finest lines. It was dedicated to Elizabeth. Life had begun to smile handsome rewards upon the Brownings.

Victorian society was very much taken with all things spiritualist. It was not enough to have command of much of the globe through Empire, they wished to know and explore wherever they could. The spirit world beckoned their interest. Browning dissented from this view believing it was all a hoax and a fraud. Elizabeth, however, was inclined to believe and this caused several disagreements between the couple.

They attended a séance by Daniel Dunglas Home, in July 1855. (Home was a famous and clamored after Scottish physical medium with the reported ability to levitate and speak with the dead). It is said that during this séance a spirit face materialised. Home then claimed it was the face of Browning's son who had died in infancy. Browning seized the 'materialisation' which turned out to be Home's bare foot. Browning had never lost a son in infancy.

After the séance, Browning wrote an angry letter to The Times, in which he said: "the whole display of hands, spirit utterances etc., was a cheat and imposture."

The Browning's time in Italy were immensely rewarding years for both their personal and professional lives. Browning encouraged her to include Sonnets from the Portuguese in her published works, these beautiful poems are undoubtedly one of the highlights of English love poetry.

Elizabeth had become quite politicised during these years. Engrossed in Italian politics (which was continuing to slowly re-unify the country), she issued a small volume of political poems entitled Poems before Congress (1860) most of which were written to express her sympathy with the Italian cause after the earlier outbreak of The Second Italian Independence War in 1859. In England they caused uproar. Conservative magazines such as Blackwood's and the Saturday Review labelled her a fanatic. She dedicated the book to her husband.

But in 1861 tragedy struck.

The couple had spent the winter of 1860–61 in Rome when Elizabeth's health deteriorated again and they returned to Florence in early June. However, these turned out to be her final weeks. Only morphine would now still the pain. She died in Browning's arms on June 29th, 1861. Browning said that she died "smilingly, happily, and with a face like a girl's .... Her last word was .... "Beautiful".

Her burial took place in the nearby Protestant English Cemetery of Florence. The local people were deeply saddened, and shops closed their doors in grief and respect.

Browning and their son were obviously devastated. Unable to bear being in Florence without Elizabeth they soon returned to London to live at 19 Warwick Crescent, Maida Vale.

As he re-integrated himself back into the London literary scene he began to finally receive the proper praise, respect and reputation that his works deserved.

Browning went on to publish Dramatis Personæ (1864), and The Ring and the Book (1868–1869). The latter, based on an "old yellow book" which told of a seventeenth-century Italian murder trial, received wide and generous critical acclaim. Although by now he was in the twilight of a long and prolific career, that had achieved some notable ups and downs, he was respected and indeed renowned for his talents and works.

In 1878, he revisited Italy for the first time since Elizabeth's death. He would return there on several further occasions but never to Florence.

Such was the esteem he was held in that The Browning Society was founded in 1881. Although he had never obtained a degree (something that set him apart from many other Victorian poets) he was now awarded honorary degrees from Oxford University in 1882 and then the University of Edinburgh in 1884.

In 1887, Browning produced the major work of his later years, Parleyings with Certain People of Importance in Their Day. Browning now spoke with his own voice as he engaged in a series of dialogues with long-forgotten figures of literary, artistic, and philosophic history. Unfortunately, both the critics and public were completely baffled by this.

On April 7th, 1889 Browning attended a dinner party at the home of his friend, the artist Rudolf Lehmann. The highlight of which was a recording made on a wax cylinder on an Edison cylinder phonograph. On the recording, which still exists, Browning recites part of How They Brought the Good News from Ghent to Aix, and can even be heard apologising when he forgets the words.

The recording was first played in 1890 on the anniversary of his death, at a gathering of his admirers, it was said to be the first time anyone's voice 'had been heard from beyond the grave'.

His last work Asolando: Fancies and Facts (1889), returned to his brief and concise lyric verse that was so popular. It was published on the day of his death on December 12th, 1889, Robert Browning was at his son's home Ca' Rezzonico in Venice.

He was buried in Poets' Corner in Westminster Abbey; his grave lies immediately adjacent to that of Alfred Tennyson.

Among the many who have publicly acknowledged their literary debt to him are Henry James, Oscar Wilde, George Bernard Shaw, G. K. Chesterton, Ezra Pound, Jorge Luis Borges, and Vladimir Nabokov.

Robert Browning - A Concise Bibliography

Here follows a list of the plays and poetry volumes published during his lifetime. Poems of particular worth are noted from within those volumes.

Pauline: A Fragment of a Confession (1833)
Paracelsus (1835)
Strafford (play) (1837)
Sordello (1840)
Bells and Pomegranates No. I: Pippa Passes (play) (1841)
        The Year's at the Spring
Bells and Pomegranates No. II: King Victor and King Charles (play) (1842)
Bells and Pomegranates No. III: Dramatic Lyrics (1842)
        Porphyria's Lover
        Soliloquy of the Spanish Cloister
        My Last Duchess
        The Pied Piper of Hamelin
        Count Gismond
        Johannes Agricola in Meditation
Bells and Pomegranates No. IV: The Return of the Druses (play) (1843)
Bells and Pomegranates No. V: A Blot in the 'Scutcheon (play) (1843)
Bells and Pomegranates No. VI: Colombe's Birthday (play) (1844)
Bells and Pomegranates No. VII: Dramatic Romances and Lyrics (1845)
        The Laboratory
        How They Brought the Good News from Ghent to Aix
        The Bishop Orders His Tomb at Saint Praxed's Church
        The Lost Leader
        Home Thoughts from Abroad
        Meeting at Night
Bells and Pomegranates No. VIII: Luria and A Soul's Tragedy (plays) (1846)
Christmas-Eve and Easter-Day (1850)
An Essay on Percy Bysshe Shelley (essay) (1852)
Two Poems (1854)
Men and Women (1855)
        Love Among the Ruins
        A Toccata of Galuppi's

www.ingramcontent.com/pod-product-compliance
Lightning Source LLC
Chambersburg PA
CBHW070111070426
42448CB00038B/2520